God's Promises and Prayers for Grief and Depression

Lawanda Walker - Tave

"Promises and Prayers for grief and depression"

Published By: LaWanda Walker-Tave

Copyright ©2024, Lawanda Walker-Tave

All rights reserved

No portion of this book may be reproduced in any form without prior permission from the copyright owner of this book .

For permission contact: Lawanda.tave2012@gmail.com

Cover and title page by: canva https://www.canva.com

All scriptures are firmly taken from the King James Bible.

Contents

Acceptance	1	Healing	51
Addiction	3	Hope	53
Adjustments	5	Identity	55
Anxiety	7	Joy	57
Assurance	9	Kindness	59
Beauty	11	Loneliness	61
Blessing	13	Life	63
Boldness	15	Loss	65
Comfort	17	Love	67
Compassion	19	Overwhelmed	69
Confidence	21	Praise	71
Confused	23	Prayer	73
Courage	25	Pride	75
Deliverance	27	Purpose	77
Depression	29	Relief	79
Doubt	31	Safety	81
Encouragement	33	Salvation	83
Eternity	35	Strength	85
Faithful	37	Stress	87
Fear	39	Support	89
Friendship	41	Trust	91
Goodness	43	Thankfulness	93
Grace	45	Understanding	95
Grief	47	Victory	97
Guilt	49	Wisdom	100

About the Author

LaWanda Walker-Tave is a compassionate wife, dedicated mother, and passionate advocate for mental health and well-being. Born and raised in Henderson, TX, LaWanda's journey through life's challenges led her to discover her calling in supporting others through their own struggles. With a heart full of empathy and a deep understanding of the human experience, she has devoted her career to guiding individuals towards healing and empowerment.

Currently residing in Longview, TX, LaWanda finds inspiration in her roles as a devoted wife to Andrew and a loving mother to her children, Jordan, Lyriah, and Jayden. Her personal experiences with grief and loss have fueled her mission to help others navigate their own journeys of overcoming adversity and finding hope amidst despair.

LaWanda's approach to overcoming grief is rooted in empathy, resilience, and faith. Drawing from her expertise as a grieving mother, she provides practical strategies, heartfelt insights, and profound wisdom to guide readers towards healing and renewal. Through her writing, LaWanda offers a beacon of light for those traversing the dark tunnels of grief, reminding them that they are not alone and that there is hope on the horizon.

With her debut self-help book, LaWanda Walker-Tave invites readers to embark on a transformative journey towards healing, resilience, and inner peace. Her words resonate with authenticity and grace, offering solace and inspiration to all who seek comfort in the midst of life's storms.

Acknowledgement:

To my Lord and Savior, Jesus Christ thank you for his infinite love and the gift of salvation.

To Andrew, thank you for being my biggest supporter and my best friend and a constant source of encourgement.

Thank you, Jayden and Lyriah, for bringing constant happiness and joy into my life.
It is an honor to be called your mom.

To Mrs. Kelly Gray
Thank you for being my spiritual mentor and friend for so many years.

To one of my best friends, Sabrina S., thank you for your support on this journey. I love you big..

Dr. Laramie J. Jackson, thank you for being my therapist, and for putting up with
me and for keeping it real - your advice has been helpful, even if it was difficult to hear sometimes.

"In memory of"
05/10/2002-02/27/2023

"I loved you your whole life and I will miss you for the rest of mine"

This book is dedicated to my oldest son,
Jordan D. Montgomery,
who recently passed away on February 27,2023, after dealing with a rare disease called aplastic anemia.
He cherished his siblings Jayden and Lyriah.
He had a passion for basketball.
He never met a stranger to know him was to love him!
Each day without you Jordan is a day closer to seeing you again.
You are loved and missed.

A word from your author:

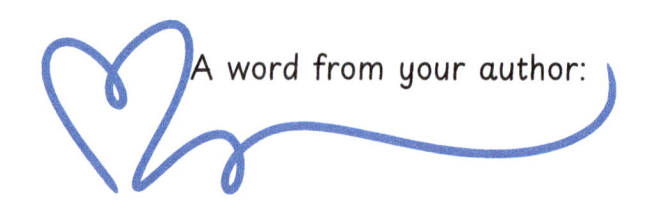

Have you ever had to take an unexpected journey and not know the end result? This book "God's Promise and Prayers for Grief and Depression" is for you. It has been a lifesaver for me as I wrote it, soothing my hurting heart with Bible verses. I had to take an unexpected journey when my son Jordan and my brother Andrew passed away ten months apart. Those two deaths took a toll on me as a mom and as a sister. I honestly didn't know how I was supposed to walk through this grief journey and be OK and still function and live. At this moment all I knew is that I was just existing. But one thing for certain, two things for sure, is that I never walked the journey of grief alone from day one. The one person that was there for me when no one else was, was my God. He loved me when I couldn't love myself. He hugged me when I wasn't huggable. When all I did was cry and I couldn't speak he was there to listen to those unspoken tears. I hope that this book will bring you a sense of hope, and peace that passes all understanding.
My prayer is
that this book will help you to get through those hard days that no one knows besides God. Your journey is just beginning.
Just know you are not alone....

Lawanda Walker - Tave

"Thoughts"

"God's Promises and Prayers for Grief and Depression"

"ACCEPTANCE"

"What shall we then say to these things?
If God be for us, who can be against us?"
Romans 8:31 KJV

"But ye are a chosen generation, a royal priesthood, an holy nation, a peculiar people; that ye should shew forth the praises of him who hath called you out of darkness into his marvellous light:"
1 Peter 2:9 KJV

"Wherefore receive ye one another, as Christ also received us to the glory of God."
Romans 15:7 KJV

"But the Lord said unto Samuel, Look not on his countenance, or on the height of his stature; because I have refused him:
for the Lord seeth not as man seeth;
for man looketh on the outward appearance, but the Lord looketh on the heart."
1 Samuel 16:7 KJV

"God's Promises and Prayers for Grief and Depression"

I express my heartfelt gratitude for Your acceptance
of me, just as I am, and not as I should be.
Dear God, it is a tremendous blessing to know that
you see me differently than anyone else.
Your greatness is unparalleled, and your choice
of me before my birth is a testament to that.
The fact that nothing can change
Your mind about me fills me with immense joy.
So glad you choose me to be me!

"PRAYER"

Dear God,
I pray that I may be a vessel for your grace and love.
May I be filled with your Spirit and embrace the
unique purpose for which you created me. Help
me to love you and others with the
same unconditional love that you shower upon us.
May I rest in the knowledge that your love for me is
unchanging and not based on my actions. May my
life be a reflection of your love and goodness.
In your precious name,
Amen

"God's Promises and Prayers for Grief and Depression"

"ADDICTION"

"There hath no temptation taken you but such as is common to man: but God is faithful, who will not suffer you to be tempted above that ye are able; but will with the temptation also make a way to escape, that ye may be able to bear it."
1 Corinthians 10:13 KJV

"Be sober, be vigilant; because your adversary the devil, as a roaring lion, walketh about, seeking whom he may devour:"
1 Peter 5:8 KJV

"All things are lawful unto me, but all things are not expedient: all things are lawful for me, but I will not be brought under the power of any."
1 Corinthians 6:12 KJV

"Submit yourselves therefore to God. Resist the devil, and he will flee from you."
James 4:7 KJV

"God's Promises and Prayers for Grief and Depression"

Certain life events can be overwhelming and relentless, but hope persists. Despite humanity's inherent fallibility, we must choose between the path of temptation and the path of God. This world presents numerous challenges, including addiction and its dire consequences, but we must persevere and prioritize a productive life. With Christ, there is always hope.

"PRAYER"

Dear God,
We come to you with hope in our hearts and pray for those who are struggling with addiction. We ask that you guide them on their journey towards healing and deliverance. May your presence be felt and your love be the source of their strength. Remove any obstacles that hinder their progress and let your grace shine upon them. We give you all the glory and praise for the transformation that is taking place in their lives.
In your precious name,
Amen

"God's Promises and Prayers for Grief and Depression"

"ADJUSTMENT"

"And be not conformed to this world: but be ye transformed by the renewing of your mind, that ye may prove what is that good,
and acceptable, and perfect, will of God."
Romans 12:2 KJV

"For let not that man think that he shall receive any thing of the Lord. A double minded man is unstable in all his ways."
James 1:7-8 KJV

"Trust in the Lord with all thine heart; and lean not unto thine own understanding. In all thy ways acknowledge him, and he shall direct thy paths."
Proverbs 3:5-6 KJV

"Be strong and of a good courage, fear not, nor be afraid of them: for the Lord thy God, he it is that doth go with thee; he will not fail thee, nor forsake thee."
Deuteronomy 31:6 KJV

"God's Promises and Prayers for Grief and Depression"

The Bible guides us to transform into the likeness and image of Jesus Christ, and to adapt and adjust accordingly. By allowing God to adjust us, he can straighten our crooked ways and smooth our rough patches, ultimately leading to a more effective life for Christ.Let us adjust what needs to be adjusted

"PRAYER"

Dear God,
I beseech you to search my heart and reveal any hidden virtues within me. Please help me to receive your adjustments with an open heart, whether they be minor attitude adjustments or more significant changes. May your guidance enable me to overcome negative emotions such as anger, hatred, and impatience, and help me to cultivate a forgiving spirit. May all these adjustments lead me towards goodness and righteousness.
In your precious name,
Amen

"God's Promises and Prayers for Grief and Depression"

"ANXIETY"

"Cast thy burden upon the Lord, and he shall sustain thee: he shall never suffer the righteous to be moved."
Psalm 55:22 KJV

"Be careful for nothing; but in every thing by prayer and supplication with thanksgiving let your requests be made known unto God."
Philippians 4:6 KJV

"For God hath not given us the spirit of fear; but of power, and of love and of a sound mind."
2 Timothy 1:7 KJV

"So that we may boldly say, The Lord is my helper, and I will not fear what man shall do unto me."
Hebrews 13:6 KJV

"God's Promises and Prayers for Grief and Depression"

God, When anxiety and uncertainty overwhelm my being, be the tranquility that stills the turmoil within me. As my Savior, you are aware of my comings and goings, my innermost thoughts, and my heart. Always remind me of who You are to me - my Defender, Healer, Savior, and Protector. No one has my back like you do. Despite the challenges, I will continue to trust in You. You are the beacon of light at the end of my fears and anxieties.

"PRAYER"

Dear God,
Thank you for being my guiding light. I humbly submit all my worries and problems to your divine feet, trusting that you are never taken by surprise. I adore you and confidently leave my burdens with you, for you because you have the wisdom to address them.
In your precious name,
Amen

"ASSURANCE"

"Hitherto have ye asked nothing in my name: ask, and ye shall receive, that your joy may be full."
John 16:24 KJV

"If we confess our sins, he is faithful and just to forgive us our sins, and to cleanse us from all unrighteousness."
1 John 1:9 KJV

"Yea, though I walk through the valley of the shadow of death, I will fear no evil: for thou art with me; thy rod and thy staff they comfort me."
Psalm 23:4 KJV

"Be careful for nothing; but in every thing by prayer and supplication with thanksgiving let your requests be made known unto God."
Philippians 4:6 KJV

"God's Promises and Prayers for Grief and Depression"

In times of need, you are the one we depend on. While humans may fail, God is the ultimate source of strength. As we begin the day, we place our trust in you to guide us. Protect us from the evil of this world and provide us with the necessary shield when we need it. Let us convert our barriers of trials into bridges of hope

"PRAYERS"

Dear God,
I pray for an unwavering trust in your presence, that I may never doubt your guidance and love. Replace my fears and doubts with the knowledge of your grace and mercy. May your thoughts be my guide through every challenge and remind me that I am yours forevermore.
In your precious name,
Amen

"God's Promises and Prayers for Grief and Depression"

"BEAUTY"

"Thou art all fair, my love; there is no spot in thee."
Song of Solomon 4:7 KJV

"The grass withereth, the flower fadeth: but the word of our God shall stand for ever."
Isaiah 40:8 KJV

"Therefore I say unto you, Take no thought for your life, what ye shall eat, or what ye shall drink; nor yet for your body, what ye shall put on. Is not the life more than meat, and the body than raiment?"
Matthew 6:25 KJV

"Favour is deceitful, and beauty is vain: but a womanthat feareth the Lord, she shall be praised."
Proverbs 31:30 KJV

When I contemplate the splendor and diversity that surrounds me, O Lord, I am filled with wonder and awe. The beauty that resides within me is a testament to your creative power, for you have crafted me with great care and precision. Let us be grateful for the way the Lord has shaped us, as we are all fashioned in His image. Our Savior has created all things, including ourselves, with beauty and the potential for greatness. May we strive to excel in all that we do, bringing glory to God in the process.

"PRAYER"

Dear God,
I want to see the beauty in everyday life, in every small thing you make. Thank you for the smile that brightens my face, even in hard times. Help me to grow in your mercy and grace, so I become more beautiful inside and out. Thank you for making all things beautiful and for the joy found in the simple things of life.
I love you, Lord.
In your precious name,
Amen

"BLESSINGS"

"God be merciful unto us, and bless us; and cause his face to shine upon us; Selah."
Psalm 67:1 KJV

"Blessed is every one that feareth the Lord; that walketh in his ways."
Psalm 128:1 KJV

"O taste and see that the Lord is good: blessed is the man that trusteth in him."
Psalm 34:8 KJV

"But my God shall supply all your need according tohis riches in glory by Christ Jesus."
Philippians 4:19 KJV

"God's Promises and Prayers for Grief and Depression"

What blessings are you grateful for? When I reflect on the numerous occasions you have blessed me, I am compelled to praise your name. Despite the challenges we face, it is easy to overlook God's blessings and goodness. However, when I count my blessings, your presence is the greatest one, and I am thankful for it. You are the source of countless gifts, and today I will look for them in everything around me. We are truly blessed beyond measure!

"PRAYER"

Dear God,
Thank you for your unwavering love and blessings upon us daily. Help us to be content with what we have and not yearn for the things we don't have. May our hearts be filled with gratitude and love for you daily. Thank you, Lord, for being our rock and refuge.
In your precious name,
Amen

"Boldness"

"The wicked flee when no man pursueth: but the righteous are bold as a lion."
Proverbs 28:1 KJV

"And for me, that utterance may be given unto me, that I may open my mouth boldly, to make known the mystery of the gospel,"
Ephesians 6:19 KJV

"Seeing then that we have such hope, we use great plainness of speech:"
2 Corinthians 3:12 KJV

"Preaching the kingdom of God, and teaching those things which concern the Lord Jesus Christ, with all confidence, no man forbidding him."
Acts 28:31 KJV

Displaying boldness can be difficult at times, but with God's support, it is attainable. Lord, you are my strength and I appreciate that. With your guidance, I can boldly face any situation that comes my way. You are a loving God! With you beside me, I don't have to be fearful or intimidated because you are my strength. Help me to remember that courage and boldness stem from my willingness to seek your assistance, not from being perfect

"PRAYER"

Dear God,
I pray for the courage to boldly face every challenge that comes my way. May my faith in you give me the strength to overcome fear and shyness, and may I be a powerful witness for your teachings. Just as you are strong and brave, I aspire to have those qualities.
In your precious name,
Amen.

"COMFORT"

"Come unto me, all ye that labour and are heavy laden, and I will give you rest."
Matthew 11:28 KJV

"Watch ye, stand fast in the faith, quit you like men, be strong."
1 Corinthians 16:13 KJV

"But they that wait upon the Lord shall renew their strength; they shall mount up with wings as eagles; they shall run, and not be weary; and they shall walk, and not faint."
Isaiah 40:31 KJV

"My brethren, count it all joy when ye fall into divers temptations;"
James 1:2 KJV

"God's Promises and Prayers for Grief and Depression"

The Lord is my source of strength and comfort in the face of sadness, disappointment, and despair. I am thankful for a Heavenly Father who offers me a safe haven, providing comfort and strength to endure trials that seem impossible to understand, and granting me peace that transcends all comprehension when my back is against the wall.

"PRAYER"

Dear God,
While we cannot control life's unpredictability, we can control our response. I pray for your comfort and peace in times of turmoil. May I also be an instrument of comfort to others in need of a warm embrace.
In your precious name,
Amen

"COMPASSION"

"And he said, I will make all my goodness pass before thee, and I will proclaim the name of the Lord before thee; and will be gracious to whom I will be gracious, and will shew mercy on whom I will shew mercy."
Exodus 33:19 KJV

"I will mention the lovingkindnesses of the Lord, and the praises of the Lord, according to all that the Lord hath bestowed on us, and the great goodness toward the house of Israel, which he hath bestowed on them according to his mercies, and according to the multitude of his lovingkindnesses."
Isaiah 63:7 KJV

"Behold, we count them happy which endure. Ye have heard of the patience of Job, and have seen the end of the Lord; that the Lord is very pitiful, and of tender mercy."
James 5:11 KJV

"They shall not hunger nor thirst; neither shall the heat nor sun smite them: for he that hath mercy on them shall lead them, even by the springs of water shall he guide them."
Isaiah 49:10 KJV

True compassion goes beyond empathy and demands action. It's a vital necessity for humanity. We can emulate Christ's example of compassion by showing kindness and understanding to all people. Compassion is an essential part of our life's purpose. Helping others not only benefits them but also has a positive impact on our lives. What can you do to show more compassion to others?

"PRAYER"

Dear God,
I am filled with gratitude for the boundless compassion you shower upon me every day. Your unwavering love transforms my life and inspires me to share that love with those around me, especially those who are suffering. The trials you place in my path are opportunities for me to grow and bring glory to your name. I love you, God, not for the blessings you bestow upon me, but for who you are - my rock, my savior, and my guiding light.
In your precious name,
Amen

"CONFIDENCE"

"For the Lord shall be thy confidence, and shall keep thy foot from being taken."
Proverbs 3:26 KJV

"So that we may boldly say, The Lord is my helper, and I will not fear what man shall do unto me."
Hebrews 13:6 KJV

"Some trust in chariots, and some in horses: but we will remember the name of the Lord our God."
Psalm 20:7 KJV

"He that trusteth in his own heart is a fool: but whoso walketh wisely, he shall be delivered."
Proverbs 28:26 KJV

Confidence is a vital quality that can help us navigate life's challenges and reach our full potential. But where does it originate? Is it something we're born with, or can it be developed through personal growth and development? As a person of faith, I believe that true confidence comes from a higher power. When we're feeling uncertain or unsure, it's important to seek guidance and support from those we trust, such as friends, family, or spiritual leaders. But ultimately, it's in the love and grace of Christ that we find the greatest source of confidence and strength. Through prayer and devotion, we can deepen our relationship with God and find the self-assurance and courage to overcome any obstacle that comes our way

"PRAYER"

Dear God,
I want to express my sincere appreciation for the confidence that You give me daily. Your unwavering support and guidance are the reason I can face each day with courage and hope. Thank you for being my solid foundation and for allowing me to come to you with boldness in prayer. You are truly my everything, and I am forever grateful for your love and grace.
In your precious name,
Amen

"God's Promises and Prayers for Grief and Depression"

"CONFUSED"

"For God is not the author of confusion, but of peace, as in all churches of the saints."
1 Corinthians 14:33 KJV

"The heart is deceitful above all things, and desperately wicked: who can know it?"
Jeremiah 17:9 KJV

"A man's heart deviseth his way: but the Lord directeth his steps."
Proverbs 16:9 KJV

"But if ye have bitter envying and strife in your hearts, glory not, and lie not against the truth."
James 3:14 KJV

"God's Promises and Prayers for Grief and Depression"

Do you find yourself struggling to navigate life's challenges, unsure of what direction to take? We've all been there, but take heart, because God is always with us. He offers clarity and guidance, not confusion. With God, you can be sure that what He sends will come with clarity, not confusion. So, let go of uncertainty and embrace the stability that comes from having a strong and unwavering God by your side.

"PRAYER"

Dear God,
Thank you for the gift of clarity. May I always seek your understanding and not lean on my own limited perspective. Help me to overcome the daily struggles that weigh me down and trust in your divine plan.
I love you and have faith in your guidance.
In your precious name,
Amen

"God's Promises and Prayers for Grief and Depression"

"COURAGE"

"Be strong and of a good courage, fear not, nor be afraid of them: for the Lord thy God, he it is that doth go with thee; he will not fail thee, nor forsake thee."
Deuteronomy 31:6 KJV

"The Lord is my light and my salvation; whom shall I fear? the Lord is the strength of my life; of whom shall I be afraid?"
Psalm 27:1 KJV

"Have not I commanded thee? Be strong and of a good courage; be not afraid, neither be thou dismayed: for the Lord thy God is with thee whithersoever thou goest."
Joshua 1:9 KJV

"For I the Lord thy God will hold thy right hand, saying unto thee, Fear not; I will help thee."
Isaiah 41:13

I am grateful for the courage I have with you, Lord. Have you ever felt like your words are falling on deaf ears? If so, perhaps seek divine guidance for the right words and the courage to minister to others. Is courage crucial to you? Thank you, Lord, for never faltering or letting go of your grip on me. When I am afraid and can't find the strength I need, I will trust in you. Thank you for your unwavering faithfulness.

"PRAYER"

Dear God,
We are grateful for the illuminated path that leads us closer to you. Please continue to guide and protect us from all obstacles and distractions that may lead us astray. Grant us the courage and strength to overcome life's challenges, and remind us of your unwavering presence during moments of weakness and self-doubt. May our faith in you deepen with each passing day, and may we always seek comfort and guidance.
In your precious name,
Amen

"God's Promises and Prayers for Grief and Depression"

"DELIVERANCE"

"The righteous cry, and the Lord heareth, and delivereth them out of all their troubles."
Psalm 34:17 KJV

"Deliver my soul, O Lord, from lying lips, and from a deceitful tongue."
Psalm 120:2 KJV

"And the Lord shall deliver me from every evil work, and will preserve me unto his heavenly kingdom: to whom be glory for ever and ever. Amen."
2 Timothy 4:18 KJV

"And even to your old age I am he; and even to hoar hairs will I carry you: I have made, and I will bear; even I will carry, and will deliver you."
Isaiah 46:4 KJV

Who is more familiar with your challenges and tribulations than you? The answer is God. When we feel like giving up due to struggles, He knows. God, You are my rock, my savior, and my guiding light. In times of weakness, I am grateful that You are the one who lifts me up, higher and stronger than my most formidable adversary.

"PRAYER"

Dear God,
We offer our thanks for your deliverance, which transcends all human understanding. You have shown us that we can trust you with every aspect of our lives, and that through the Holy Spirit, we can overcome any obstacle. May our hearts be filled with gratitude and our lives be a reflection of your love and grace.
In your precious name,
Amen

"DEPRESSION"

"And the Lord, he it is that doth go before thee; he will be with thee, he will not fail thee, neither forsake thee: fear not, neither be dismayed."
Deuteronomy 31:8 KJV

"Fear thou not; for I am with thee: be not dismayed; for I am thy God:I will strengthen thee; yea, I will help thee; yea, I will uphold thee with the right hand of my righteousness."
Isaiah 41:10 KJV

"Who hath delivered us from the power of darkness, and hath translated us into the kingdom of his dear Son:"
Colossians 1:13 KJV

"The Lord also will be a refuge for the oppressed, a refuge in times of trouble."
Psalm 9:9 KJV

Are you feeling lost in the darkness of depression? Remember that God is always holding onto you, even when you feel too weak to hang on. He will catch you every time you fall and provide the strength you need to keep going. Don't let depression keep you hidden in the shadows – let God's love shine on you and bring you back into the light. Identify the root causes of your depression and trust that God will help you overcome them, just as He has always done in the past.

"PRAYER"

Dear God,
Please grant me your divine assistance when I find myself in darkness, unable to see a way out and with my back against the wall. May your strength be my source of empowerment when I feel weak and unable to find my footing. Continue to hold me close when I consistently fall and fill my mind with positive thoughts, displacing any depressive ones.
I love You, God.
In your precious name,
Amen

"DOUBT "

"But let him ask in faith, nothing wavering. For he that wavereth is like a wave of the sea driven with the wind and tossed."
James 1:6 KJV

"Jesus answered and said unto them, Verily I say unto you, If ye have faith, and doubt not, ye shall not only do this which is done to the fig tree, but also if ye shall say unto this mountain, Be thou removed, and be thou cast into the sea; it shall be done."
Matthew 21:21 KJV

"Keep yourselves in the love of God, looking for the mercy of our Lord Jesus Christ unto eternal life."
Jude 1:21 KJV

"And immediately Jesus stretched forth his hand, and caught him, and said unto him, O thou of little faith, wherefore didst thou doubt?"
Matthew 14:31 KJV

"God's Promises and Prayers for Grief and Depression"

The notion that you are the only one who has ever questioned God's existence is a common misconception. In reality, numerous individuals, including prominent figures such as Adam, Eve, Moses, and John the Baptist, have grappled with similar doubts. It is important to understand that you have the ability to choose how you respond to these doubts. Will you allow worry, fear, and doubt to consume you, or will you turn to God for guidance and support? God has promised to deliver us if we reach out to Him, and one way to overcome doubt is by strengthening your relationship with Christ through His word and prayer, even in the midst of uncertainty

"PRAYER"

Dear God,
I pray that You take this doubt away from me and fill my heart with peace. Help me to see myself as you see me and understand the purpose that You have given me. Thank you, Jesus, for breaking down the doors of my unbelief and reminding me that all things are possible through you.
In your precious name,
Amen

"God's Promises and Prayers for Grief and Depression"

"ENCOURAGEMENT"

"These things I have spoken unto you, that in me ye might have peace. In the world ye shall have tribulation: but be of good cheer; I have overcome the world."
John 16:33 KJV

"And we know that all things work together for good to them that love God, to them who are the called according to his purpose."
Romans 8:28 KJV

"Have not I commanded thee? Be strong and of a good courage; be not afraid, neither be thou dismayed: for the Lord thy God is with thee whithersoever thou goest."
Joshua 1:9 KJV

"Wherefore comfort yourselves together, and edify one another, even as also ye do."
1 Thessalonians 5:11 KJV

How are you encouraging others? Divine encouragement conveys God's truth and hope in a way that strengthens others to follow him. Don't be surprised by this statement, but God is the ultimate source of encouragement. Encouragement is the act of instilling confidence. It's like fuel for the soul, providing the strength to persevere through difficult times. A kind word can rekindle a person's self-confidence and remind them of their worth, that they truly matter. Remember, you matter too, even if it's just with God.

"PRAYER"

Dear God,
I come before you with a humble heart, seeking your divine assistance in all aspects of my life. May your words be a balm to my soul, healing me of all fears and doubts, and granting me the courage to boldly face life's trials. May your wisdom guide me on my journey, and your strength sustain me when I feel weak. May I always find peace in your loving arms.
In your precious name,
Amen

"ETERNITY"

"To every thing there is a season, and a time to every purpose under the heaven:"
Ecclesiastes 3:1 KJV

"And they said, Believe on the Lord Jesus Christ, and thou shalt be saved, and thy house."
Acts 16:31 KJV

"Before the mountains were brought forth, or ever thou hadst formed the earth and the world, even from everlasting to everlasting, thou art God."
Psalm 90:2 KJV

"But I would not have you to be ignorant, brethren, concerning them which are asleep, that ye sorrow not, even as others which have no hope."
1 Thessalonians 4:13 KJV

Eternity is a state of timeless existence, unchanging and infinite in nature. It offers us a glimpse into the goodness and grace that heaven embodies, where there will be no sickness or sin. Let us be real thankful for the promise of spending eternity with God in such a paradise. Not to mention we get to spend eternity with our loved ones who have gone before us.

"PRAYER"

Dear God,
You are our hope and our comfort. You have given us the gift of eternal life through Jesus, and we are forever grateful. Help us to live with purpose and to share the good news of your love and grace with a world that desperately needs it. May our lives be a reflection of your glory and may we always seek to bring you joy and honor.
In your precious name,
Amen

"FAITHFUL"

"But the fruit of the Spirit is love, joy, peace, longsuffering, gentleness, goodness, faith,"
Galatians 5:22 KJV

"Let us hold fast the profession of our faith without wavering; (for he is faithful that promised;)"
Hebrews 10:23 KJV

"Fear none of those things which thou shalt suffer: behold, the devil shall cast some of you into prison, that ye may be tried; and ye shall have tribulation ten days: be thou faithful unto death, and I will give thee a crown of life."
Revelation 2:10 KJV

"Moreover it is required in stewards, that a man be found faithful."
1 Corinthians 4:2 KJV

We cannot overlook God's faithfulness. When we doubt His presence, let us recall how He has been with us through every situation, even when we were too blind to see Him. I am grateful for God's unwavering love and resolve towards us. As a child of the King, I will hold on to his hand during my darkest moments. We must trust in God's ability to do what we know He will do.
Thank you, God, for your faithfulness.

"PRAYER"

Dear God,
Your faithfulness is a shining light in my life. You have shown me your unwavering commitment through every up and down, every triumph and struggle. Forgive me for the times I have doubted your plan and forgotten your love. Thank you for being a faithful God who always has my best interests at heart.
In your precious name,
Amen

"God's Promises and Prayers for Grief and Depression"

"FEAR "

"What time I am afraid, I will trust in thee."
Psalm 56:3 KJV

"Have not I commanded thee? Be strong and of a good courage; be not afraid, neither be thou dismayed: for the Lord thy God is with thee whithersoever thou goest."
Joshua 1:9 KJV

"The Lord is my light and my salvation; whom shall I fear? the Lord is the strength of my life; of whom shall I be afraid?"
Psalm 27:1 KJV

"The fear of the Lord is the beginning of wisdom: and the knowledge of the holy is understanding."
Proverbs 9:10 KJV

What areas of your life can you trust in the Lord's guidance and protection right now? Remember that fear comes in many forms, but love and faith can overcome any obstacle. Let go of the fear that holds you back and embrace the purpose God has designed for you. The only one we should fear is our Heavenly Father, who is also our protector and guide.

"PRAYER"

Dear God,
Thank you for being our shelter from the storms of life, so that we may not be overwhelmed by its small details. Thank you for being our rock, our hope, and our trusted ally. As we lean on you, our hearts find solace and security in your unfailing love.
We love You, God!
In your precious name,
Amen

"FRIENDSHIP"

"A man that hath friends must shew himself friendly: and there is a friend that sticketh closer than a brother."
Proverbs 18:24 KJV

"A friend loveth at all times, and a brother is born for adversity."
Proverbs 17:17 KJV

"This is my commandment, That ye love one another, as I have loved you. Greater love hath no man than this, that a man lay down his life for his friends."
John 15:12-13 KJV

"And the Lord turned the captivity of Job, when he prayed for his friends: also the Lord gave Job twice as much as he had before."
Job 42:10 KJV

Good friends are essential in our lives, just like the anointing oil that brings forth the sweet fragrance of our heavenly Father. Having genuine friends is vital, as they will be there for us through thick and thin. Can you recall a time when you embodied the role of a true friend? Our friendships are temporary and have a predetermined time limit, much like seasonal workers. However, our friendship with Jesus is everlasting and unwavering.

"PRAYER"

Dear God,
I pray for discernment to pick my friends wisely. I ask that you open my eyes to see people who need me to be a friend to them. Help me to also be the friend I desire and long to have in my own life. thank you, for creating the gift of friendship and blessing me with godly relationships through different friendships. Each friend has a purpose in my life.
In your precious name,
Amen

"God's Promises and Prayers for Grief and Depression"

"GOODNESS"

"O give thanks unto the Lord; for he is good; for his mercy endureth for ever."
1 Chronicles 16:34 KJV

"The Lord is good, a strong hold in the day of trouble; and he knoweth them that trust in him."
Nahum 1:7 KJV

"Thou art good, and doest good; teach me thy statutes."
Psalm 119:68 KJV

"And they sang together by course in praising and giving thanks unto the Lord; because he is good, for his mercy endureth for ever toward Israel. And all the people shouted with a great shout, when they praised the Lord, because the foundation of the house of the Lord was laid."
Ezra 3:11 KJV

Your goodness, Oh God, knows no bounds. All good things originate from You. Let us seek the good things that our Savior has prepared for us, no matter how small they may be. Keep in mind that God's goodness is a promise to us. To be more aware of His goodness, meditate on His word both day and night. Think of ways to demonstrate the goodness of God to others.

"PRAYER"

Dear God,
I pray for your divine guidance as I immerse myself in your holy scriptures. May your goodness and love be reflected in every situation and aspect of my life. Help me to worship you with reverence and gratitude for your boundless mercy and grace.
In your precious name,
Amen

"GRACE"

"And of his fulness have all we received, and
grace for grace."
John 1:16 KJV

"And if by grace, then is it no more of works: otherwise grace is
no more grace. But if it be of works, then is it no more grace:
otherwise work is no more work."
Romans 11:6 KJV

"And now, brethren, I commend you to God, and to the word
of his grace, which is able to build you up, and to give you
an inheritance among all them which are sanctified."
Acts 20:32 KJV

"Thou in thy mercy hast led forth the people which thou
hast redeemed: thou hast guided them in thy strength
unto thy holy habitation."
Exodus 15:13 KJV

How does God's grace manifest in your world? God's grace is undeserving favor. It cannot be earned; it is a free gift from God. Grace is giving someone a chance and the ability to make a mistake without punishment or forgiveness. It is also an act of kindness. We are grateful for our Savior's grace when we make mistakes. We can show grace by forgiving everyone unconditionally, as God has forgiven us through Christ. God's grace is demonstrated through His love.

"PRAYER"

Dear God,
I place today in your capable hands, asking for your shield of protection to cover my life. Thank you for the power of grace that you bestow upon me. May we open our hearts to your grace, allowing it to work in us and grant us peace in your presence.
In your precious name,
Amen

"GRIEF"

"And God shall wipe away all tears from their eyes; and there shall be no more death, neither sorrow, nor crying, neither shall there be any more pain: for the former things are passed away."
Revelation 21:4 KJV

"It is of the Lord's mercies that we are not consumed, because his compassions fail not."
Lamentations 3:22 KJV

"He healeth the broken in heart, and bindeth up their wounds."
Psalm 147:3 KJV

"Verily, verily, I say unto you, If a man keep my saying, he shall never see death."
John 8:51 KJV

Grief is a difficult and emotional journey that can be overwhelming. It is important to recognize that grief is rooted in love, but it can be challenging to navigate. Seeking divine guidance and support can offer comfort and help during this difficult time. Remember that God is always present, especially when the emotional weight becomes too much to bear. By allowing God to heal your heart and guide you through the grieving process, you can find peace and understanding

"PRAYER"

Dear God,
I am grateful for your unwavering love and grace in my life. When I am overwhelmed, may your strength, mercy, and love cover me like a warm embrace. Thank you for being my constant companion, guiding me through life's darkest moments. I am humbled by your power and grateful for your presence.
In your precious name,
Amen

"GUILT"

"For godly sorrow worketh repentance to salvation not to be repented of: but the sorrow of the world worketh death."
2 Corinthians 7:10 KJV

"Yet if any man suffer as a Christian, let him not be ashamed; but let him glorify God on this behalf."
1 Peter 4:16 KJV

"As far as the east is from the west, so far hath he removed our transgressions from us."
Psalm 103:12 KJV

"In thee, O Lord, do I put my trust; let me never be ashamed: deliver me in thy righteousness."
Psalm 31:1 KJV

Christ's atonement covered all sins, past, present, and future, freeing believers from guilt and shame. By acknowledging our failures, we can break free from guilt's hold and embrace our worth in Christ. When we confess our sins, He purifies us and cleanses our conscience. To deal with guilt, we should confess, seek divine guidance for improvement, trust God's promises, reflect on His Word, and pray for His intervention.

"PRAYER "

Dear God,
I acknowledge that I have fallen short of your glory, not only in my actions but also in my thoughts and words.
Help me to rise above my limitations and become the best version of myself. Thank you for your unwavering love and for understanding my heart's deepest desires.
In your precious name,
Amen

"God's Promises and Prayers for Grief and Depression"

"HEALING"

"For I the Lord thy God will hold thy right hand, saying unto thee, Fear not; I will help thee."
Isaiah 41:13 KJV

"Bless the Lord, O my soul, and forget not all his benefits: Who forgiveth all thine iniquities; who healeth all thy diseases; Who redeemeth thy life from destruction; who crowneth thee with lovingkindness and tender mercies;"
Psalm 103:2-4 KJV

"He healeth the broken in heart, and bindeth up their wounds."
Psalm 147:3 KJV

"Heal me, O Lord, and I shall be healed; save me, and I shall be saved: for thou art my praise."
Jeremiah 17:14 KJV

On occasion, our healing requires divine intervention in areas that are not immediately visible. As specified in Jesus' teachings, we are encouraged to tend to those who are sick. By imploring God for comprehensive healing and leveraging His inherent knowledge of our design, we can contribute effectively to the restorative process, while relying on His strength and trusting in His capacity to guideus through the journey.

"PRAYER"

Dear God,
I come before you with an open heart and mind, allowing your healing energy to flow through me like a river, washing away all pain and suffering. I trust in your divine power to heal me on all levels, body, mind, and spirit. May your peace and love envelop me and guide me towards wholeness.
In your precious name,
Amen

"God's Promises and Prayers for Grief and Depression"

"HOPE"

"My brethren, count it all joy when ye fall into divers temptations;"
James 1:2 KJV

"For I know the thoughts that I think toward you, saith the Lord, thoughts of peace, and not of evil, to give you an expected end."
Jeremiah 29:11 KJV

"Therefore I will look unto the Lord; I will wait for the God of my salvation: my God will hear me."
Micah 7:7 KJV

"Rejoicing in hope; patient in tribulation; continuing instant in prayer;"
Romans 12:12 KJV

During times of adversity, my hope is founded in you, God.
When my circumstances seem dire, I look to you for strength
and guidance. While I may not know what the future holds,
I trust that you will guide me through every challenge.
My hope is in you and not in human abilities.

"PRAYER"

Dear God,
I am grateful that you will never leave me nor forsake me.
In the midst of my trials, I seek your face for hope and strength.
The Bible assures me that you are the source of all hope, a gift
that you freely give. May I always have the confidence to trust
and hope in you.
In your precious name,
Amen

"IDENTITY

"Wherefore receive ye one another, as Christ also received us to the glory of God."
Romans 15:7 KJV

"Therefore if any man be in Christ, he is a new creature: old things are passed away; behold, all things are become new."
2 Corinthians 5:17 KJV

"So God created man in his own image, in the image of God created he him; male and female created he them."
Genesis 1:27 KJV

"For our conversation is in heaven; from whence also we look for the Saviour, the Lord Jesus Christ:"
Philippians 3:20 KJV

"God's Promises and Prayers for Grief and Depression"

It's common to want to be someone God doesn't intend us to be. However, God created each of us as unique individuals, and our identity is of utmost importance to Him. Our primary objective should be to emulate God in every way possible. By allowing God to teach us, we can become more like Him. What does God see when He looks at you? How does He perceive you? Your identity plays a significant role in determining your sense of belonging , which in turn affects your confidence and overall well-being.

"PRAYER"

Dear God,
I pray for the wisdom to see myself through your eyes. Help me to reject the negative self-talk that can cloud my vision and instead, may I see the beauty and potential that you see in me. Remind me that I am fearfully and wonderfully made, a true masterpiece of your creation. When I feel lost and uncertain, may I find comfort in the knowledge that I am your greatest work of art, a true reflection of your love and grace.
In your precious name,
Amen

"God's Promises and Prayers for Grief and Depression"

"JOY"

"My brethren, count it all joy when ye fall into divers temptations;"
James 1:2 KJV

"Now the God of hope fill you with all joy and peace in believing, that ye may abound in hope, through the power of the Holy Ghost."
Romans 15:13 KJV

"And ye now therefore have sorrow: but I will see you again, and your heart shall rejoice, and your joy no man taketh from you."
John 16:22 KJV

"This is the day which the Lord hath made; we will rejoice and be glad in it."
Psalm 118:24 KJV

Joy can often be found in the simple moments of life. Various circumstances can bring joy or sorrow to one's heart. Recognize that joy is a choice and it has the power to spread, so share it with those who seem to lack it. When we choose joy, it's hard not to smile.

"PRAYER"

Dear God,
I pray that you fill me with unspeakable joy, guiding me towards a life of happiness and peace, even in the darkest moments. May your divine presence always remind me that I am never alone, and may your Holy Spirit bring me unwavering peace.
In your precious name,
Amen

"God's Promises and Prayers for Grief and Depression"

"KINDNESS"

"And be ye kind one to another, tenderhearted, forgiving one another, even as God for Christ's sake hath forgiven you."
Ephesians 4:32 KJV

"Charity suffereth long, and is kind; charity envieth not; charity vaunteth not itself, is not puffed up,"
1 Corinthians 13:4 KJV

"He that hath pity upon the poor lendeth unto the Lord; and that which he hath given will he pay him again."
Proverbs 19:17 KJV

"My little children, let us not love in word, neither in tongue; but in deed and in truth."
1 John 3:18 KJV

"God's Promises and Prayers for Grief and Depression"

How can we bring kindness to those around us? In my opinion, kindness is sharing the best part of our hearts with others. It's about stepping out of our comfort zone to make others feel important. I believe kindness is part of our DNA. It creates a sense of belonging and helps reduce isolation. Remember, kindness matters and it's intentional.

"PRAYER"

Dear God,
I thank You for Your graciousness towards me. Please direct me to those who need to witness kindness. Remind me to radiate kindness through my smiles, friendships, and Your word.
Thank You for granting me the gift of kindness.
In Your precious name,
Amen

"LONELINESS"

"When my father and my mother forsake me, then the Lord will take me up."
Psalm 27:10 KJV

"Be strong and of a good courage, fear not, nor be afraid of them: for the Lord thy God, he it is that doth go with thee; he will not fail thee, nor forsake thee."
Deuteronomy 31:6 KJV

"And the Lord God said, It is not good that the man should be alone; I will make him an help meet for him."
Genesis 2:18 KJV

"He healeth the broken in heart, and bindeth up their wounds."
Psalm 147:3 KJV

Loneliness can have a significant impact on stress levels. It involves being alone or isolated, leading to feelings of rejection and worthlessness. However, it's important to remember that we can trust in God, our forever friend in Christ, during these difficult times. If loneliness is affecting you, seek support
from your Savior to navigate these challenges.

"PRAYER"

Dear God,
I am humbled by Your unwavering presence in my life. May I always look to You for solace when I feel alone. Thank You for your reassuring embrace and for being a rock when everyone else turns against me. May I be a beacon of your light, shining hope and kindness on those who are lonely and in need of a friend.
In your name,
Amen

"God's Promises and Prayers for Grief and Depression"

"LIFE"

"Jesus saith unto him, I am the way, the truth, and the life: no man cometh unto the Father, but by me."
John 14:6 KJV

"For the wages of sin is death; but the gift of God is eternal life through Jesus Christ our Lord."
Romans 6:23 KJV

"The thief cometh not, but for to steal, and to kill, and to destroy: I am come that they might have life, and that they might have it more abundantly. I am the good shepherd: the good shepherd giveth his life for the sheep."
John 10:10-11 KJV

"And the Lord God formed man of the dust of the ground, and breathed into his nostrils the breath of life; and man became a living soul."
Genesis 2:7 KJV

What is the most remarkable aspect of the life that God has blessed you with? I am so grateful for God's unwavering love and guidance. He never promised that the path would be easy, but He assured us that He would never leave us nor forsake us. God meets us in our darkest moments and transforms our struggles into a stairway to triumph. Your life has a purpose, and your testimony can inspire others and bring glory to God.

"PRAYER"

Dear God,
I come before you with a heart full of praise and gratitude for your boundless mercies. Thank you for the gift of life and the renewed strength you provide daily. Thank you for your unwavering companionship and guidance. May I always remember to trust in your sovereignty and lean on your infinite wisdom, especially during life's darkest moments.
In your precious name,
Amen

"God's Promises and Prayers for Grief and Depression"

"LOSS"

"My flesh and my heart faileth: but God is the strength of my heart, and my portion for ever."
Psalm 73:26 KJV

"And ye now therefore have sorrow: but I will see you again, and your heart shall rejoice, and your joy no man taketh from you."
John 16:22 KJV

"And God shall wipe away all tears from their eyes; and there shall be no more death, neither sorrow, nor crying, neither shall there be any more pain: for the former things are passed away."
Revelation 21:4 KJV

"Have not I commanded thee? Be strong and of a good courage; be not afraid, neither be thou dismayed: for the Lord thy God is with thee whithersoever thou goest."
Joshua 1:9 KJV

Loss can be overwhelming, but remember that God's compassion and guidance are always available to us. He understands our pain and is there to offer us comfort and support, even when it seems like no one else does. Trust in His plan and lean on Him during difficult times. With faith and perseverance, we can navigate the most challenging situations and emerge stronger and more resilient.

"PRAYER"

Dear God,
I am grateful for the opportunity to pour out my grief before you. You are a loving father who embraces me with open arms, offering hope, peace, and healing for my broken heart. Restore in me the joy that only you can give, and help me to trust.
In your precious name,
Amen

"LOVE"

"Let all your things be done with charity."
1 Corinthians 16:14 KJV

"And above all these things put on charity, which is the bond of perfectness."
Colossians 3:14 KJV

"Greater love hath no man than this, that a man lay down his life for his friends."
John 15:13 KJV

"With all lowliness and meekness, with longsuffering, forbearing one another in love;"
Ephesians 4:2 KJV

"God's Promises and Prayers for Grief and Depression"

The affection God has for us is exemplified in our interactions with others. His love is unique and encompasses everything. No problem is too great for His love to solve, and it serves as a balm for soothing pain. I am grateful that His love is what motivates me to move forward. The price we pay for loving someone is grief when we lose them. Take your pain and sorrow to God, for He is love. The Holy Spirit will offer you solace and peace.

"PRAYER"

Dear God,
I humbly ask that you continue to shower me with your boundless love, especially in times of grief and sorrow. May your divine mercy embrace us during moments of struggle and confusion. Let your radiant light shine through me, that others may witness your glory and be inspired. Thank you for your infinite love and grace, demonstrated daily in our lives.
In your precious name,
Amen

"God's Promises and Prayers for Grief and Depression"

"OVERWHELMED"

"Hear my cry, O God; attend unto my prayer. From the end of the earth will I cry unto thee, when my heart is overwhelmed: lead me to the rock that is higher than I. For thou hast been a shelter for me, and a strong tower from the enemy."
Psalm 61:1-3 KJV

"When my spirit was overwhelmed within me, then thou knewest my path. In the way wherein I walked have they privily laid a snare for me. I looked on my right hand, and beheld, but there was no man that would know me: refuge failed me; no man cared for my soul. I cried unto thee, O Lord: I said, Thou art my refuge and my portion in the land of the living."
Psalm 142:3-5 KJV

"But they that wait upon the Lord shall renew their strength; they shall mount up with wings as eagles; they shall run, and not be weary; and they shall walk, and not faint."
Isaiah 40:31 KJV

"Jesus Christ the same yesterday, and to day, and for ever."
Hebrews 13:8 KJV

Feeling overwhelmed by the demands of life is a common experience, but know that you don't have to face it alone. Tap into your inner strength and resilience, and trust that God is always available to offer guidance and comfort. Remember that even Christ faced similar challenges, so it's okay to feel overwhelmed sometimes. Focus on your well-being and let God help you navigate these difficult times.
It's okay to not be okay.

"PRAYER"

Dear God,
Please help me to calm the storm growing in my mind and heart. Lord, I need to feel your peace. When life is too much to handle you are there. I look forward to tomorrow.
I love you, God.
In your precious name,
Amen

"PRAISE"

"Blessed be God, even the Father of our Lord Jesus Christ, the Father of mercies, and the God of all comfort; Who comforteth us in all our tribulation, that we may be able to comfort them which are in any trouble, by the comfort wherewith we ourselves are comforted of God."
2 Corinthians 1:3-4 KJV

"Out of the same mouth proceedeth blessing and cursing. My brethren, these things ought not so to be."
James 3:10 KJV

"God is a Spirit: and they that worship him must worship him in spirit and in truth."
John 4:24 KJV

"Then Job arose, and rent his mantle, and shaved his head, and fell down upon the ground, and worshipped, And said, Naked came I out of my mother's womb, and naked shall I return thither: the Lord gave, and the Lord hath taken away; blessed be the name of the Lord."
Job 1:20-21 KJV

With God, there are no mistakes or surprises. He meticulously plans and executes all aspects of our lives. During trials, we praise Him, gaining strength and hope from His sovereignty. To praise God in difficult times, we can:
1) study the Bible,
2) listen to uplifting music,
3) communicate openly with our savior.

"PRAYER"

Dear God,
I praise You for Your eternal goodness and greatness in my life. May my life always reflect Your glory. Teach me to walk in Your ways, respecting who You are to me. All my praise and glory will always lift you up. I will always sing praises and glorify You.
In your precious name,
Amen

"PRAYER"

"And all things, whatsoever ye shall ask in prayer, believing, ye shall receive."
Matthew 21:22 KJV

"Therefore I say unto you, What things soever ye desire, when ye pray, believe that ye receive them, and ye shall have them."
Mark 11:24 KJV

"Confess your faults one to another, and pray one for another, that ye may be healed. The effectual fervent prayer of a righteous man availeth much."
James 5:16 KJV

"Hear me when I call, O God of my righteousness: thou hast enlarged me when I was in distress; have mercy upon me, and hear my prayer."
Psalm 4:1 KJV

"God's Promises and Prayers for Grief and Depression"

Prayer is our personal means of communication with God. Although He is aware of everything that happens in our world, He still desires to hear from us. Whom can you pray for today? Prayer is significant because it allows us to communicate with God, bring our problems to Him, and offer praises. Through prayer, we can develop a closer relationship with God, and when we pray, blessings follow. Don't hesitate to bring your prayers to God; He is eager to hear from you. When we pray for others, it helps to heal our hearts. I have discovered that prayer is more than just a platform for making requests; it is a sanctuary of serenity and solace. My problems do not accompany me to the throne of grace, nor are they welcome there. The embrace of the Father is a place of comfort.

"PRAYER"

Dear God,
Grant me a clear mind when I come to you in prayer.
Help me communicate with you effectively. I'm grateful
that you don't require perfection in my prayers.
You know my heart,
and I appreciate the gift of prayer that connects us.
In your precious name,
Amen

"God's Promises and Prayers for Grief and Depression"

"PRIDE"

"When pride cometh, then cometh shame: but with the lowly is wisdom."
Proverbs 11:2 KJV

"Pride goeth before destruction, and an haughty spirit before a fall."
Proverbs 16:18 KJV

"But let every man prove his own work, and then shall he have rejoicing in himself alone, and not in another."
Galatians 6:4 KJV

"For the day of the Lord of hosts shall be upon every one that is proud and lofty, and upon every one that is lifted up; and he shall be brought low:"
Isaiah 2:12 KJV

Our Savior has expressed his disdain for pride (Proverbs 8:13). It can impede one's blessings and acquisition of essential knowledge and skills for success. It may even restrict one's actions. Have you examined your pride levels? There are three types of pride: dignity, superiority, and arrogance. Which one do you exhibit? To overcome pride, redirect your focus to God, seek forgiveness for prideful sins, and seek divine assistance in modifying behaviors that glorify you and not Him.

"PRAYER"

Dear God,
I ask for Your forgiveness regarding pride. Help us recognize that everything we have comes from You and we can do nothing by ourselves. Please remove the temptation of pride from our heart and mind, and let us be more like You, Lord, and less like ourselves.
In your precious name,
Amen

"PURPOSE"

"I will cry unto God most high; unto God that performeth all things for me."
Psalm 57:2 KJV

"Every man according as he purposeth in his heart, so let him give; not grudgingly, or of necessity: for God loveth a cheerful giver. And God is able to make all grace abound toward you; that ye, always having all sufficiency in all things, may abound to every good work: (As it is written, He hath dispersed abroad; he hath given to the poor: his righteousness remaineth for ever."
2 Corinthians 9:7-9 KJV

"He hath shewed thee, O man, what is good; and what doth the Lord require of thee, but to do justly, and to love mercy, and to walk humbly with thy God?"
Micah 6:8 KJV

"But ye are a chosen generation, a royal priesthood, an holy nation, a peculiar people; that ye should shew forth the praises of him who hath called you out of darkness into his marvellous light:"
1 Peter 2:9 KJV

Have you discovered the meaning and purpose of your life? Seeking guidance from the divine creator, we can align our personal goals with His grand plan. To do so, immerse yourself in scripture, seek wise counsel, and ask God for wisdom and discernment. Your passions often indicate your purpose, but it may require some self-reflection to recognize it. Don't worry if you're struggling to find your purpose; it may be due to a lack of focus on yourself and God's plan. Trust that He has a plan for you, and don't try to understand His ways; He knows best.

"PRAYER"

Dear God,
I am grateful for the journey You have taken me through. Your guiding hand has prepared me for the great things You have in store for me. Thank You for giving my life meaning and purpose. May I always remember that You have a plan to prosper me, not to harm me, and that plan gives me hope and a future.
In your precious name,
Amen

"God's Promises and Prayers for Grief and Depression"

"RELIEF"

"And this is the confidence that we have in him, that, if we ask any thing according to his will, he heareth us:"
1 John 5:14 KJV

"Seek the Lord and his strength, seek his face continually."
1 Chronicles 16:11 KJV

"Wherein he hath abounded toward us in all wisdom and prudence;"
Ephesians 1:8 KJV

"I pray not that thou shouldest take them out of the world, but that thou shouldest keep them from the evil."
John 17:15 KJV

"God's Promises and Prayers for Grief and Depression"

Relief is a feeling of reassurance and relaxation that follows the release from anxiety or distress. God tells us to come to Him in prayer when overwhelmed and to seek peace that surpasses all understanding.
What can you give to God to carry for you?

"PRAYER"

Dear God,
I ask for complete peace in my body, mind, and spirit. Please heal and remove all sources of grief, stress, and sorrow in my life. Walk ahead of me and keep my mind at peace.
Thank you for the relief you will provide.
In your precious name,
Amen

"SAFETY"

"I will both lay me down in peace, and sleep: for thou, Lord, only makest me dwell in safety."
Psalm 4:8 KJV

"Put on the whole armour of God, that ye may be able to stand against the wiles of the devil."
Ephesians 6:11 KJV

"Where no counsel is, the people fall: but in the multitude of counsellors there is safety."
Proverbs 11:14 KJV

"Teaching them to observe all things whatsoever I have commanded you: and, lo, I am with you alway, even unto the end of the world. Amen."
Matthew 28:20 KJV

"God's Promises and Prayers for Grief and Depression"

According to the Bible, God is our refuge and strength. Our strength comes from God, who listens to our requests and protects us. God's love for us is so great that He wants to ensure our safety in every situation, even when no one else will keep us safe. Don't believe anyone who tells you that God isn't ready to protect you because that is untrue

"PRAYER"

Dear God,
I am so thankful for the gift of prayer. Today, I come to You with faith that You will shield my loved ones, our minds, and our home from harm. Your presence guarantees their safety, whether they are with me or not. Thank You for Your unwavering love and protection.
In your precious name,
Amen

"God's Promises and Prayers for Grief and Depression"

"SALVATION"

"Not by works of righteousness which we have done, but according to his mercy he saved us, by the washing of regeneration, and renewing of the Holy Ghost;"
Titus 3:5 KJV

"Jesus saith unto him, I am the way, the truth, and the life: no man cometh unto the Father, but by me."
John 14:6 KJV

"And brought them out, and said, Sirs, what must I do to be saved? And they said, Believe on the Lord Jesus Christ, and thou shalt be saved, and thy house. And they spake unto him the word of the Lord, and to all that were in his house. And he took them the same hour of the night, and washed their stripes; and was baptized, he and all his, straightway."
Acts 16:30-33 KJV

"For sin shall not have dominion over you: for ye are not under the law, but under grace."
Romans 6:14 KJV

"God's Promises and Prayers for Grief and Depression"

When you hear about the plan of salvation, how do you respond? God's word teaches that salvation is a gift from God that we can't earn. It comes through faith and is available to everyone, but not everyone will accept it. Have you shared the gospel with others and told them about the reality of heaven and hell?

"PRAYER"

Dear God,
I am grateful for the gift of salvation. Thank you for sending your son to die for me and others. Please give me the courage to share your gift with others. Thank you for the cross and for being a loving God.
In your precious name,
Amen

"God's Promises and Prayers for Grief and Depression"

"STRENGTH"

"The Lord is my strength and song, and he is become my salvation:
he is my God, and I will prepare him an habitation;
my father's God, and I will exalt him."
Exodus 15:2 KJV

"Be strong and of a good courage, fear not, nor be afraid of them:
for the Lord thy God, he it is that doth go with thee;
he will not fail thee, nor forsake thee."
Deuteronomy 31:6 KJV

"God is my strength and power: and he maketh my way perfect.
He maketh my feet like hinds' feet: and setteth me upon my high places."
2 Samuel 22:33-34 KJV

"Seek the Lord and his strength, seek his face continually."
1 Chronicles 16:11 KJV

When you need the strength to overcome challenges, remember that God's strength is limitless. Trust in Him and draw from His endless supply. Don't rely on your own strength, but look to God for the energy to keep going. He will take you further than you ever thought possible.

"PRAYER"

Dear God,
I am grateful for the strength you give us every day.
Without you, we would be weak and rely on our own strength.
Thank you for being faithful and meeting me where I am as
your child. Thank you for loving and caring for
me like I'm your only child.
In your precious name,
Amen

"God's Promises and Prayers for Grief and Depression"

"STRESS"

"Take therefore no thought for the morrow: for the morrow shall take thought for the things of itself. Sufficient unto the day is the evil thereof."
Matthew 6:34 KJV

"Come unto me, all ye that labour and are heavy laden, and I will give you rest."
Matthew 11:28 KJV

"Peace I leave with you, my peace I give unto you: not as the world giveth, give I unto you. Let not your heart be troubled, neither let it be afraid."
John 14:27 KJV

"The Lord shall fight for you, and ye shall hold your peace."
Exodus 14:14 KJV

"God's Promises and Prayers for Grief and Depression"

Stress is pervasive in our lives and can impact our relationship with Christ. When stressed, we may neglect prayer and Bible reading. However, God wants us to come to Him and let Him carry our burdens. Stress can affect every aspect of our lives.
Let's not let it overtake us.

"PRAYER"

Dear God,
Thank you for calming my mind during stressful times. Please help me not to over stress on things outside of my control. Thank you for being a refuge when I feel alone and overwhelmed. Thank you for loving me even in my weariness and for carrying my burdens, allowing me to breathe a little easier.
I love you deeply.
In your precious name,
Amen

"SUPPORT"

"And if one prevail against him, two shall withstand him; and a threefold cord is not quickly broken."
Ecclesiastes 4:12 KJV

"For God is not unrighteous to forget your work and labour of love, which ye have shewed toward his name, in that ye have ministered to the saints, and do minister."
Hebrews 6:10 KJV

"Give to him that asketh thee, and from him that would borrow of thee turn not thou away."
Matthew 5:42 KJV

"Distributing to the necessity of saints; given to hospitality."
Romans 12:13 KJV

"God's Promises and Prayers for Grief and Depression"

Having a faithful friend like Jesus is truly wonderful. It's great to have someone to rely on during difficult times. God's support is unmatched and we should be grateful for his guidance. Having a supportive friend is a great feeling and we should cherish those moments. God's ways are always better than ours and we should trust in his plan

"PRAYER"

Dear God,
I am grateful for your unwavering love and support. Your ways are higher than mine, and I am thankful that I can always come to you. I love that I can lean into your arms and feel your embrace, as if I am your only child.
I love you, God!
In your precious name,
Amen

"God's Promises and Prayers for Grief and Depression"

"TRUST"

"And they that know thy name will put their trust in thee: for thou, Lord, hast not forsaken them that seek thee."
Psalm 9:10 KJV

"Some trust in chariots, and some in horses: but we will remember the name of the Lord our God."
Psalm 20:7 KJV

"Behold, God is my salvation; I will trust, and not be afraid: for the Lord Jehovah is my strength and my song; he also is become my salvation."
Isaiah 12:2 KJV

"When thou passest through the waters, I will be with thee; and through the rivers, they shall not overflow thee: when thou walkest through the fire, thou shalt not be burned; neither shall the flame kindle upon thee."
Isaiah 43:2 KJV

"God's Promises and Prayers for Grief and Depression"

What does trust mean to you? When faced with life's uncertainties, I place my trust in God. When the path ahead is shrouded in darkness, I will continue to trust in Him. God desires our trust, not in people or circumstances. Instead of burdening others with our troubles, we should seek solace in Him. God is aware of our struggles and invites us to trust in His guidance. The devil's intention is to make us doubt God's presence, but we must remember that God has never abandoned us. He has been with us through every trial, mistake, heartbreak, and unspoken struggle. Let Him guide you through life's challenges

"PRAYER"

Dear God,
Help me to trust you with every decision and lean on you with all my heart. Thank you for your faithfulness, protection, care, and provision. Forgive me for questioning my circumstances when I should trust you more. Show me how to trust you more.
In your precious name,
Amen

"THANKFULNESS"

"Giving thanks always for all things unto God and the Father in the name of our Lord Jesus Christ;"
Ephesians 5:20 KJV

"O give thanks unto the Lord, for he is good: for his mercy endureth for ever."
Psalm 107:1 KJV

"We give thanks to God always for you all, making mention of you in our prayers;"
1 Thessalonians 1:2 KJV

"Blessed be the Lord, because he hath heard the voice of my supplications."
Psalm 28:6 KJV

Gratitude is about acknowledging the valuable and meaningful aspects of our lives, which we have been given by God. We should cultivate a habit of thankfulness until it becomes second nature, expressing appreciation for the countless blessings we have received.
We are truly blessed..

"PRAYER"

Dear God,
I thank you for the blessings you've given me. You've provided more than I could imagine. Please help me see your blessings, including your love and mercy. Thank you for being my faithful father, who brings stability and strength. I'm thankful that you are my savior.
In your precious name,
Amen

"UNDERSTANDING"

"And to love him with all the heart, and with all the understanding, and with all the soul, and with all the strength, and to love his neighbour as himself, is more than all whole burnt offerings and sacrifices."
Mark 12:33 KJV

"And the peace of God, which passeth all understanding, shall keep your hearts and minds through Christ Jesus."
Philippians 4:7 KJV

"And we know that the Son of God is come, and hath given us an understanding, that we may know him that is true, and we are in him that is true, even in his Son Jesus Christ. This is the true God, and eternal life."
1 John 5:20 KJV

"God's Promises and Prayers for Grief and Depression"

God wants us to understand that life wasn't promised to be easy, but He did promise to walk beside us on our journey. We can approach Him with our questions. Thank you for your patience, God. How can we seek to understand Him more? He knows our thoughts before we do and is always with us, even in difficult situations. We can turn to Him with confidence when things go wrong, as He knows how to handle all situations, big or small.

"PRAYER"

Dear God,
I don't understand the things happening around me right now. They make me feel helpless, afraid, and weak. However, I know that You are God and my circumstances are in Your hands. I trust You completely. Thank You for understanding my life.
In your precious name,
Amen.

"VICTORY"

"For whatsoever is born of God overcometh the world:
and this is the victory that overcometh the world, even our faith."
1 John 5:4 KJV

"But thanks be to God, which giveth us the victory
through our Lord Jesus Christ."
1 Corinthians 15:57 KJV

"Some trust in chariots, and some in horses: but we
will remember the name of the Lord our God."
Psalm 20:7 KJV

"Nay, in all these things we are more than conquerors
through him that loved us."
Romans 8:37 KJV

"God's Promises and Prayers for Grief and Depression"

This is our winning season. With Jesus, we will triumph! Victory is ours in Jesus, and we must not give up. Jesus wins every battle. Prayer and perseverance bring answers to our prayers, and God will come through. Our vocabulary matters, and God sees
our struggles. He wants us to trust Him for victory and glory. Let's strive for victory in Jesus daily.

PRAYER"

Dear God,
I am more than a conqueror. Although I may fall, You are always there to lift me up. As Your child, I am confident in Your power and presence, especially during setbacks and disappointments. May I always see Your victory and claim it for myself, daily moving forward,
In Your holy name,
amen.

"WISDOM"

"With the ancient is wisdom; and in length of days understanding. With him is wisdom and strength, he hath counsel and understanding."
Job 12:12-13 KJV

"And unto man he said, Behold, the fear of the Lord, that is wisdom; and to depart from evil is understanding."
Job 28:28 KJV

"The law of the Lord is perfect, converting the soul: the testimony of the Lord is sure, making wise the simple. The statutes of the Lord are right, rejoicing the heart: the commandment of the Lord is pure, enlightening the eyes."
Psalm 19:7-8 KJV

"If any of you lack wisdom, let him ask of God, that giveth to all men liberally, and upbraideth not; and it shall be given him."
James 1:5 KJV

"God's Promises and Prayers for Grief and Depression"

Wisdom is the quality of being wise, in harmony with the creative order and God's redemptive work. It involves trusting in God, rather than our own understanding, and seeing things from his perspective. Wisdom also enables us to make accurate judgment. We should strive to recognize God's wisdom daily as we pray, study, and follow him.

"PRAYER"

Dear God,
I am grateful for the gift of wisdom. I ask for your help and understanding in making important decisions, and I seek your wisdom and direction daily. Thank you again for this gift.
In your precious name,
Amen.

In need of a Christian counselor to help you navigate through life storms? I would highly recommend Legendary Consulting. You don't have to walk through the storms of life alone. "Get help for whatever needs help."